LET'S GO APPLE PICKING!

By Cliff Griswold

Gareth Stevens
PUBLISHING

Please visit our website, www.garethstevens.com. For a free color catalog of all our high-quality books, call toll free 1-800-542-2595 or fax 1-877-542-2596.

Library of Congress Cataloging-in-Publication Data

Griswold, Cliff.
  Let's go apple picking! / Cliff Griswold.
      pages cm. — (Fun in fall)
  Includes index.
  ISBN 978-1-4824-1781-4 (pbk.)
  ISBN 978-1-4824-1782-1 (6 pack)
  ISBN 978-1-4824-1780-7 (library binding)
  1. Apples—Juvenile literature. I. Title. II. Series: Griswold, Cliff. Fun in fall.
  SB363.G67 2015
  634'.11—dc23

                              2014022973

First Edition

Published in 2015 by
Gareth Stevens Publishing
111 East 14th Street, Suite 349
New York, NY 10003

Copyright © 2015 Gareth Stevens Publishing

Editor: Ryan Nagelhout
Designer: Nicholas Domiano

Photo credits: Cover, pp.1, 17 Adie Bush/Cultura/Getty Images; p. 5 Irina Fischer/Shutterstock.com; p. 7 Gunnar Pippel/Shutterstock.com; p. 9 Alexander Chaikin/Shutterstock.com; p. 11 Fotokostic/Shutterstock.com; p. 13 PhotoSGH/Shutterstock.com; p. 15 Matteo Festi/Shutterstock.com; p. 19 Lee Prince/Shutterstock.com; p. 21 David Hanlon/Shutterstock.com; p. 23 margouillat photo/Shutterstock.com.

Printed in the United States of America

CPSIA compliance information: Batch #CW15GS: For further information contact Gareth Stevens, New York, New York at 1-800-542-2595.

Contents

Apple Time 4

Up the Tree 14

Take a Bite. 20

Words to Know 24

Index. 24

I love apples.

I go apple picking.
It is lots of fun.

Apples grow on trees.

I go to an apple farm. Farmers grow apples there!

There are many rows of trees.

My dad uses a ladder.

I grab an apple off a tree.

I fill a basket
with apples.
A big basket
is called a bushel.

My sister Lisa
likes apples, too.
She takes a big bite!

My mom makes us
apple pie!

Words to Know

 apple pie    basket    ladder

Index

apple pie 22   ladder 14

bushel 18   trees 8, 12, 16